101

TWO-LETTER WORDS

101
TWO-LETTER
WORDS

STEPHIN MERRITT

Illustrated by
ROZ CHAST

W. W. NORTON & COMPANY
NEW YORK · LONDON

For information about permission to reproduce
selections from this book, write to Permissions,
W. W. Norton & Company, Inc.,
500 Fifth Avenue, New York, NY 10110

For information about special discounts for
bulk purchases, please contact W. W. Norton Special Sales
at specialsales@wwnorton.com or 800-233-4830

Manufacturing through Asia Pacific Offset
Book design through Chin-Yee Lai
Production manager: Julia Druskin

ISBN 978-0-393-24019-1

W. W. Norton & Company, Inc.
500 Fifth Avenue, New York, N.Y. 10110
www.wwnorton.com

W. W. Norton & Company Ltd.
Castle House, 75/76 Wells Street, London W1T 3QT

1 2 3 4 5 6 7 8 9 0

INTRODUCTION

In my day job as a rock star I sit around a lot in airports, lobbies, green rooms, and hotels, waiting for unpredictable amounts of time—time that can't be spent on anything useful. So what I generally do is pull out my phone and play Scrabble or Words With Friends.

I'm a fairly good player, for a musician. But I can never remember all the two-letter words, without which such word games are clunky and awkward. So some time ago I started writing little poems as mnemonic devices. After a few I thought I'd better write all of them down, and how better to do that than to write a book? I never finish anything without a deadline anyway. I bought myself some plain white three-by-five cards, lined on one side, blank on the other—which unfortunately come in packs of one hundred—and sat around in bars and cafes writing poems for the 101 two-letter words admissible in Scrabble. I then invested in some double-sided tape and taped all the cards in a big grid up on the wall.

As with songwriting, some of these poems just popped out—I wrote the one for "ye" while crossing Fifth Avenue—and some took more than a year and many revisions. I had tried writing many totally different poems for "si," when I happened to see a billboard in Catskill, New York, advertising a doctor who treats frequent urination in elderly women, just when I was trying to give "ma" more to do.

Having grown up on Edward Gorey's faux Victoriana, I started out in slavish imitation. But it became clear that my book needed to be as modern as "yo" and "za," as Scottish as "ae" and "oe," as occult as "bo" and "od," and have prosody loose enough for deliberate sins at "oy" and "xi." (I also grew up loving Richard Brautigan, and I kept trying to squeeze in his memorable character Trout Fishing in America Shorty; but no dice.)

The Vampire Dog who haunts these pages was inspired by the late Irving Berlin Merritt, my rock star Chihuahua. Several of these poems were written with Irving happily asleep in my shirt; the grid of three-by-five cards was taped above his little heated dog bed. He was a grand old dog of fourteen, wobbly but dignified, when he died while I was correcting the final proofs. *I hear, and obey!*

—*Stephin Merritt*

101

TWO-LETTER

WORDS

There are two kinds of lava: aa
and pahoehoe.
Aa is more jagged, and
pahoehoe flowy.

AB

The perfect ab requires you
to do something called a "crunch."
But I prefer to linger
over this delicious lunch.

AD

Place an ad today, and tell
the world you've love to give.
Tomorrow, too! The world has all
the memory of a sieve.

Ae is "one" in Scots English
("Twa brothers at ae scule").
Ae and ae is twa, but ye
ken that, for ye're nae fool.

AG

Ag is agriculture, only
faster, which is better.
Ag is punk rock! Do it
in an orange mohair sweater.

AH

When your dentist says, "Say 'ah,'"
say "ah," and don't be mum.
Soon you'll get the anesthetic.
If not? Bite her thumb.

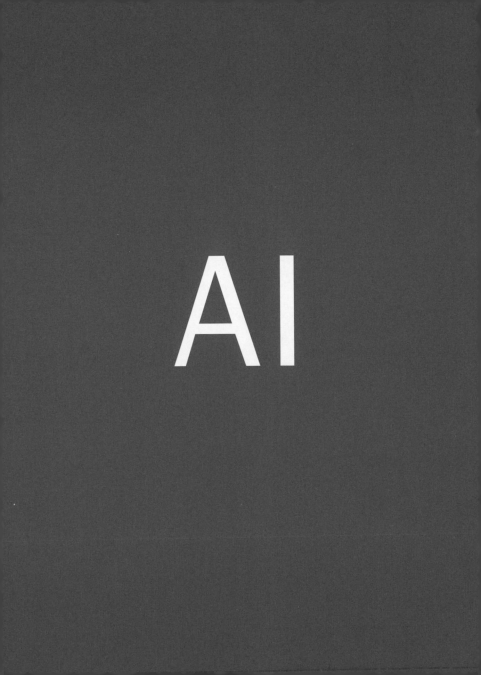

The ai, a threatened three-toed sloth
found only in Brazil,
munches on leaves and sleeps in trees.
I hope it always will.

AL

The al, or vomit fruit, is used
for cancer, pain, and rash;
it lowers your cholesterol,
and then puts out the trash.

AM

"I think, therefore I am," declared
Descartes, while he was living.
That thought remains, while he does not . . .
which causes some misgiving.

An androgyne from Anchorage
annoyed an anthropologist
and suffered injuries that sent
him to the gynecologist.

AR

"Ar, ar, ar!" the pirates say.
Ar is their favorite letter.
All of them say "Ar!" all day,
but parrots say it better.

AS

As I Lay Dying, William Faulkner's
seventh novel, made him.
He got some cash, a Nobel sash,
and trashy ladies laid him.

At Attitash's Alpine Slide,
they fling you off a hill.
At worst, you'll have a heart attack;
at best, you will be ill.

"Aw, that puppy sure is cute.
Please, can we take him home?"
The victims of the Vampire Dog
could fill a hefty tome.

AX

Was Lizzie Borden guilty? Strange,
the ax was never found.
Still, Lizzie never married;
people heard her name and . . . frowned.

AY

What all in favor say is "ay,"
while those agin say "nay."
But those in thrall to Vampire Dog
say, "I hear, and obey."

The ba is basically a bird,
but with a human head;
it represents your soul
(if you're Egyptian, and you're dead).

BE

"Be yourself," all thinkers say;
how odd they think alike.
"Be yourself," says Lao Tzu;
"Be yourself," says Wilhelm Reich.

BI

The bi orientation is
the happiest of all.
If only they could bottle it
and sell it at the mall.

Bo means "friend," if you're in Scotland.
Will ye be my bo?
No? Then I shall put to sea;
to see the ai I go.

BY

By the by, these poems are
all copyright by me.
You can use them too—by law—
there's just a little fee.

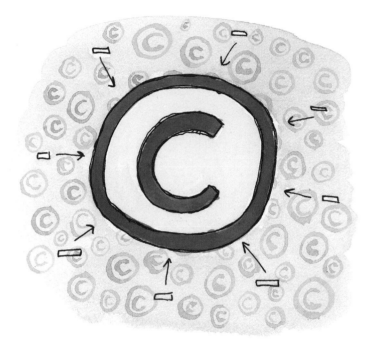

DE

De means "of," or "from," in names
like Cruella de Vil.
It's fun to use in drag-name games;
to wit: Ova de Hill.

Do re mi fa so la ti do:
Sound like secret code?
It's what we call the major scale,
or the Ionian mode.

Ed works for the board of ed.
(That's short for education.)
He's dead bored at the board of ed,
but that's his occupation.

ED

Ef starts that four-letter word
all children love repeating;
they scream it, jumping up and down,
until they get a beating.

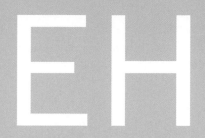

Eh? Speak up, young whippersnapper!
Eh? You must be joking;
and stop making those silly faces.
Oh wait. . . . Are you choking?

Chicago's el train glides, not 'neath
the city, but above it.
(We also have an L train in New York.
We do not love it.)

EM

Em dashes—this just in!—are used
to interrupt a thought;
the use of them is subtle—ha!—and
it cannot be taught.

EN

En dashes are the short ones, used:
–to indicate a range,
–for hyphens, bullet points, or sudden
endings: Danger! Dange–

ER

Er, I don't know what to say.
There's been some kind of error.
Why am I here, up on this stage,
in ermine and in terror?

ES

Es begins my given name;
which I have always hated,
and had to use absurd nicknames
with everyone I've dated.

Fritz
Freetz
FRITZO
ZEPPO
BEPPO
BEPS
Bappera
EPPERS
MR. EPPERS
Zid
P-ZIDDY
HALE-BOPP
H-B
Garth

Eat, or get et. On this alone
all animals agree.
(But I ain't et an animal
since 1983.)

Sometimes one feels frisky, and
one wants to sex one's ex.
Best to try it first with a
Tyrannosaurus rex.

"Fa," sings Father, "la la la,"
driving the family crazy.
He's never learned another song,
because he's fackin' lazy.

FE

Fe is iron; everybody
needs a little fe;
get a little fe inside you
once or twice a day.

Go: a subtle game of skill,
with stones of black and white.
One game can go on until
the middle of the night.

HA

Ha! ha! ha! Your hat maker
must have some sense of humor.
That hat looks like a wedding cake
with a malignant tumor.

HE

Pa's a he and Ma's a she
and Trevor is a tranny;
we're not sure what to call him now.
We used to call him Granny.

HI

Hi, which means "aloha"
on the mainland cold and gray,
can also mean Hawai'i,
where we sing and dance all day.

"Hm!" Her Majesty harrumphed.
"We do not like that song.
Go east a few hectometers,
and live among the Hmong!"

HO

"Ho ho ho," says old Saint Nick.
But saint for what, exactly?
Mayhap for hopping round the world,
and getting back intactly.

ID

Id: the source of primal drives,
like power, lust, and money;
those urges other people have,
so tragic, and so funny.

IF

If I had a hammer . . . Wait:
Why ever would Pete Seeger
lack a hammer?
Not as if his royalties were meager.

In my inbox is an
invitation to go out;
but going out is out.
I'm staying in, and getting stout.

IS

"Is You Is or Is You Ain't
My Baby" sold a million,
and not by being played at any
debutante's cotillion.

IT

It Came from Outer Space—
that pinnacle of '50s sci-fi—
is best seen at the drive-in,
in 3-D (not over Wi-Fi).

JO

Back in Scotland, jo means "sweetheart."
Will you be my jo?
Yes? Oh, joy! Come kiss me now
beneath the mistletoe.

KA

Your ka, or walking spirit,
needs a mummy, or—kaput!
So mummify yourself. Start now!
Begin with either foot.

KI

Ki, life force, is also spelled
as "qi," which seems more thrilling;
but ki extends more easily,
to kisses, kings, and killing.

LA

In La-La Land, the Lamborghinis
languish on the 5, tra la;
a traffic jam can last until
there's no one left alive, tra la.

Please, no Chinese water torture!
I confess it freely:
One li is, like, .3 miles;
a mile is roughly three li.

LO

Lo and behold! The universe
is all around us, now.
Sometimes it's so beautiful
that one can only bow.

Ma gets blamed for everything,
like every other ma.
Pa, meanwhile, is on a pub crawl,
skanking to the ska.

ME

Me and Ma, Mimi and Mo,
we got along so well,
till Mimi got her muumuu;
now our life's a living hell.

MI

"Mi, mi, mi, mi, mi, mi," Mimi sings,
to warm her throat.
Mimi is, she claims,
an opera singer, quote unquote.

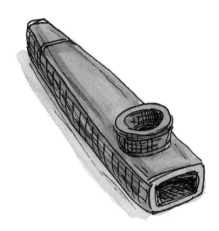

MM

"Mm" is what you sing while humming
into your kazoo.
What was that? You don't have a kazoo?
What's wrong with you?

A mo is two times half a mo—
or moustache, in Australia—
or hemidemisemiquaver,
in Sesquipedalia.

On Yasujiro Ozu's grave
is written only: mu.
It means "nothing" in Japanese;
nothing in English, too.

MY

"My kingdom for a horse," Richard
the Third is heard to say.
In my humble opinion, it's
the *only* Shakespeare play.

NA

If e'er a man of brevity
existed, he's the Scot.
It ain't just "ae" for "any";
he says "na" instead of "not."

Ne is born, if you're a man;
if you're a woman, nee.
It's just like what a horse says,
but it's spelt a different way.

No, No, Nanette, a musical
from 1924,
can still set those toes tapping:
"Tea for Two" is in the score.

NU

Nu denotes neutrino, which means
"little neutral one";
these are formed in nuclear
reactions on the sun.

The od was that mesmeric force
we now know isn't there;
like God and mod, it had its day,
then *pfft!* into thin air.

OE

Oe: a tiny island (often
teeming with amoebae);
or, in Scotland, a grandchild,
like granddad's oe Phat Phoebe.

Of (rhymes with dove), a useful word
for amorous versifiers,
is in the Poet's toolbox 'neath
the needle-nosèd pliers.

OH

Oh, followed by some harmless word,
can be an oath, or curse:
Oh, cheesemongers! Oh, folk art!
Oh, Chicago Bears! Oh, verse!

Oi is cockney for "hey there,"
or punk rock made by skinheads
and listened to by disaffected
youth and racist pinheads.

OM

"Om," the hippies chant,
inside their geodesic dome.
They owe all their happiness
to analgesic om.

ON

On and on, the Autobahn
goes, right into Berlin;
the nightlife there? Beyond compare!
Come out! Come on! Come in!

'Twas op art killed abstraction,
letting painters use a ruler;
'cause once you have a ruler,
hyperrealism's cooler.

When the song is written,
and I'm adding stuff for fun,
I recall my helpful
little motto: OR, IT'S DONE.

os

Os: a spine of gravel dropped
by long-gone giggly glaciers
playing in their sandbox, leaving
scribbles and erasures.

"Ow," says Pa, as Ma jumps up
and down upon his head.
"Take one deep breath and count to—
Ow! Is it something I said?"

OX

Trixie was the ox princess.
She ruled the happy oxen
until a rival dosed her with
a nasty neurotoxin.

OY

Oy gevalt! Oy vey! I often
wish I spoke Yiddish;
but then I'd have to eat chopped liver,
and gefilte fish.

Pa paws Paolo from Paducah
sometimes in the loo.
Ma paws Withnail, an ai
she rescued from the zoo.

People say it's like a mouth,
the Hebrew letter pe.
It isn't, though, and I don't care
two pence what people say.

PI

Rock star of the numbers,
with its own eccentric fandom,
pi is like the world itself,
both infinite and random.

QI

Qi, in Chinese medicine:
vitality, or breath;
say it "chee," as in "Say cheese!"
Its opposite is death.

RE

Re: about, in memos.
Rays: how microwaves make pork.
Re: the second scale note.
Ray's: all pizza in New York.

"Sh," says the librarian,
"people are trying to read.
And turn that goddamn cellphone off,
before I make you bleed."

SI

Si: the same as ti, the seventh
note of do re mi . . .
Ma can drink a sea of tea
but then she has to pee.

So-so soup makes someone somewhere sad.
So choose ingredients
to make so-so soup socko!
(And not solely for expedience.)

TA

Ta means either "Here's your drink"
or "This one's free," depending
on which side of the pond you're on,
and whether Ma's bartending.

Ti is called the leading tone,
because it leads to do;
and anything that leads to dough
is something you should know.

To Toto, Oz and Kansas must
look pretty much alike.
In Oz, the witch is on a broom;
in Kansas, on a bike.

Uh, this isn't going well . . .
It isn't you, it's me . . .
Instead of saying how we feel,
we fester silently.

UM

Um, I don't know what you mean.
I'm sorry to keep mum,
but when I see your face, Uma,
I'm struck completely dumb!

Un is one two-letter word
that causes some dissension;
for some say it's an English word,
and some say it's a French un.

UN

UP

Up from an unhallowed grave
the Vampire Dog arises;
now Chihuahua, now Great Dane—
a master of disguises.

US

Us is me and Gus, driving
our bus across the land;
when we die, just bury us
together, hand in hand.

UT

Time was, the French sang "ut re mi"
(instead of "do," put "ut");
but "ut" was so unmemorable,
the French do "do" now too.

WE

"And how are we today?" wheedles
that horrible new nurse.
"We are not amused," I snap.
Then I repeat this verse.

Wo is me! (And woe, as well.)
I've spilt my wonton soup
on my new worsted woolen suit.
Wow, I'm a nincompoop.

XI

Xi: fourteenth Greek letter,
or fourteenth one in a line;
like, the great great great great great great
  great great great great grandson
of the Son of Frankenstein.

The xu, one hundredth of a dong,
is hardly worth one's while;
it never bought much bubblegum,
and now it's out of style.

YA

Ya means "you"—ya think? do ya?—
in contexts less than formal;
pooh-poohed by talking poodles,
but for yakking yaks it's normal.

YE

O ye of little faith: You're right!
There's nothing to believe in.
Go run and tell your ma and pa,
and say it came from Stephin.

The country folk say "howdy-do"
but here in town, it's "yo";
they'll say it in the country too
in twenty years or so.

ZA

So Ma and Pa pick at their za
with faces grim and stony.
Ma munches on the crunchy crust,
and Pa, the pepperoni.

ABOUT THE AUTHORS

With his band the Magnetic Fields, **STEPHIN MERRITT** has written, produced, and recorded ten albums, including *69 Love Songs*, which made Best of the Year lists in the *New York Times*, *Spin*, *LA Times*, and *Washington Post* and was named one of the 500 best albums of all time by *Rolling Stone*.

Merritt has performed as part of Lincoln Center's "American Songwriters" series and at BAM's "Next Wave of Song," mounted an Off-Broadway stage musical of Neil Gaiman's *Coraline*, and composed the score for the Academy Award–nominated film *Pieces of April* and for *Eban and Charley*. He has also composed incidental music for the audio books of *A Series of Unfortunate Events* by Lemony Snicket and subsequently released the album *Songs from A Series of Unfortunate Events*.

This is his first book.

ROZ CHAST has been a regular contributor of cartoons to *The New Yorker* since 1978.

Her cartoons, which have also been published in *Scientific American*, the *Harvard Business Review*, *Redbook*, and *Mother Jones*, have been collected in *What I Hate*, *Theories of Everything*, and *The Party After You Left*. She also illustrated *The Alphabet from A to Y, with Bonus Letter, Z*, the bestselling children's book by Steve Martin. Her most recent book is *Can't We Talk About Something More Pleasant?* (Bloomsbury), a memoir about her parents.